# TALISMAN
# ORACLE

By Nora Paskaleva

Copyright © 2023 U.S. GAMES SYSTEMS, INC.

All rights reserved. The illustrations, cover design, and contents are protected by copyright. No part of this booklet may be reproduced in any form without permission in writing from the publisher, except by a reviewer who wishes to quote brief passages in connection with a review written for inclusion in a magazine, newspaper or website.

First Edition

10 9 8 7 6 5 4 3

Made in China

Published by
U.S. GAMES SYSTEMS, INC.
179 Ludlow Street
Stamford, CT 06902 USA
www.usgamesinc.com

This deck is dedicated to you—the reader! There is no one like you! You are the most important part of this deck, and you are the true magic that makes it work.

Be the one to direct your destiny!

# ACKNOWLEDGMENT

*I would like to express my special thanks to my wonderful family and friends.*

*To my kids, Mila and Evan— you are the greatest gift from the Universe and every day around you is a blessing!*

*I would like to thank my parents and especially my sister who will always be my rock and a person I look up to.*

*I want to thank the team at U.S. Games Systems, Inc. who helped me finalize this project and was there to share many tough and joyous moments of my life.*

*Thank you!*

# CONTENTS

Introduction ............................................... 7

How to Use the Deck ............................. 8

Charging your Talisman Cards ............. 10

The Threefold Law ................................. 12

Sigils & Sacred Geometry ...................... 12

Visualization & Meditation ................... 13

Affirmations ............................................ 14

Talisman Cards & Religion ................... 15

Toxic Positivity vs. Genuine Positivity ... 15

Using the Cards with Tarot Readings ... 16

Spreads .................................................... 17

The Cards ................................................ 19

About the Creator ................................ 109

Symbols ................................................ 110

Astrological Symbols ........................... 111

# INTRODUCTION

Talisman Oracle is based on the principle that the power of intention is strong enough to bring us good luck. Everyone encounters rough moments in their lives and we seek comfort to protect ourselves from the unknown or things we cannot control. Talismans are powerful tools that strengthen the power of our beliefs, which manifests into a desired outcome. They serve to guide our thoughts, empower us to take actions towards our goals, and form healthy new habits. Talismans amplify our own energy and establish an aura of positivity. An optimistic outlook on life doesn't mean that we will never experience pain or that no harm will ever come in our lives. Rather, it is about feeling confident that we will be fine no matter how things turn out. This type of attitude makes it easier to adjust our sails no matter which way the wind blows. Talisman Oracle cards are here to help you invite that energy around you and the people you love. May this deck bring you hope, peace of mind, and positive energy. Each card has been enchanted with a powerful incantation, a blessing to protect you and help you realize your dreams.

# How to Use the Deck

You can use the Talisman Oracle in two ways—as a regular oracle deck with messages for you, or you can use each card to create your own talisman. If you have questions or wish to examine a particular situation, draw a single card or use the suggested spreads in this guidebook.

Though all the design elements on the cards were created to strengthen the meaning of the card, the sigils extracted and highlighted in this guidebook are the main symbol that contains the potent energy of each card. For your convenience, the enlarged versions of the sigils are shown here alongside the card and its description. If you want to create a talisman, start by picking a card of personal interest. You can use the vellum paper included with your deck to outline the sigil graphic provided. Your drawing doesn't have to be perfect; the more abstract and unique the look, the more interesting and powerful your talisman design will be. You can add your own embellishments, color and symbols for good luck. Once the drawing is done, fold the paper an odd number of times. Insert it in a locket or simply carry it in your purse or pocket.

To strengthen the talisman's power, create your own sigils and designs and spend some time meditating on the topic of your choice. A variety of symbol options are also available on pages 110–111. Carrying your talisman with you will help deepen your intuition. It will change your thoughts' frequency, and you will soon begin to see more signs that will lead you toward your goals. If you prefer to create your talisman as an altar piece, you can add other auspicious elements such as feathers, stones, shells, glitter or flowers. Check the Talisman Power section for each card to find the best use for the specific talisman image.

# Charging your Talisman Cards

When you first open the deck, take a few minutes each day to meditate on a specific interest. Imagine that the cards serve to embody your intentions. If you believe in angels, protectors, spirits, or ancestors, imagine their energy surrounding the cards. You want to form a subconscious bond with the invisible matter that supports the image on the card. When you create the drawing, it should become the physical representation of your intention, wish, or positive emotion like love, confidence, bravery, etc. This visual connection strengthens the positive vibration and helps align your mental frequency. The power of talismans is as strong as the intent we form. Very similar to a battery, they are charged and drained periodically. Talismans can lose their effectiveness noticeably over time. When you see that happening, you can go back to drawing the energy in the form of meditation, prayer, or a simple ritual of your liking. You can redraw the talisman symbol and discard the old one. Talismans are very personal, so everyone has to form their own connection with them. Personalizing your drawings is a great way to set your intentions. Some people like to add color or experiment with different textures. You can also take advantage of events such as full moons, waxing moons, eclipses, equinoxes or special holidays to recharge your talismans, but again, let your intuition guide you.

You can carry your talismans close to you when you need them or just use them periodically as an inspiration or motivation for fulfilling your wish.

Every card comes with a special message that helps you free your spirit and focus on your purpose and the desired end result.

When your Talisman card has done its magic, remember to send a message of gratitude towards the universe and its vast powers. Staying thankful when good things happen in life is a wonderful way to keep karma on your side, and it's a step closer to mindful living.

# THE THREEFOLD LAW

As you become more confident and comfortable using the cards, remember the Threefold Law—whatever energy you put out into the world (positive or negative), it will be returned three times. This principle could simply be seen as choosing to be kind to yourself, to all of nature's creatures, and to the universe.

> *"For every one step that you take in the pursuit of higher knowledge, take three steps in the perfection of your own character."*
> —Rudolf Steiner

# SIGILS & SACRED GEOMETRY

Some of the cards have geometric patterns and sigil designs that were purposefully chosen to strengthen the power of the Talisman cards. Sacred geometry is a universal pattern rooted in the fundamental structure and templates of life in the universe. It exists because it's the most profound and efficient way to preserve energy, and it's all around us. Sigils are a way to identify and strengthen your intent. They are like secret messages that remind you to refocus your energy. When you are using a Talisman card, you can try to redraw some of the sigils and geometric shapes yourself. That may help you focus on the essence of the card.

# Visualization & Meditation

The Talisman Power sections offer a concise visualization or guidance for every card. These are available for your convenience, but you can choose to create your own mind-images and practices. Visualizations are very effective ways to create an empowering mindset. The more information you can feed the brain and the more vivid the experience, the more compelling the results. Visualizations can include imagining smell, hearing a warm voice from a loved one, or even tasting delicious food. Focusing your attention on positive scenarios and seeing things going well for you can all lead to more positive thoughts and feelings. On the other hand, meditation is excellent for finding balance when struggling with scattered thoughts, stress, and unwanted emotional interference. Meditation is a form of discipline that keeps us grounded and focused on the present moment.

## AFFIRMATIONS

Affirmations are another way to elevate your spirit and rewire your brain's subconscious beliefs that negatively impact your actions. To effectively use affirmations, they have to be said at a time when you have the greatest access to your subconscious mind. Similar to hypnosis, when your brain is in a theta state of sleep, your mental inhibitions are down, and you're more susceptible to influence. Thus, affirmations are most effective right before falling asleep and right as we are waking up. As the window of opportunity we have is quite short, it's best to use short sentences in the present tense that do not contain negations.

# Talisman Cards & Religion

You can use Talisman cards regardless of what religion you practice. Think of them as a way of opening the conversation with your God or Gods, similar to a prayer. You could also see them as a tool assisting you when seeking a blessing, protection, or love. If you are more spiritual than religious, you can use them as a way to connect to the universe, your subconscious mind, and the ultimate inner truth.

# Toxic Positivity vs. Genuine Positivity

Sometimes people try to force positivity in order to manifest abundance, but it's not that easy. Forced positivity can be incredibly toxic and harmful. The very power of a positive mindset is embedded in the process of self-evaluation, growth and shadow work. Knowing yourself, shedding fears and old crippling beliefs and establishing new boundaries is not always a pleasant process but is one that builds our internal compass. Genuine positivity is rooted in self-trust, knowing our authentic self and developing self-worth. Toxic positivity, on the other hand, is about avoidance and bulldozing negative emotions. It's crucial to be mindful of the difference.

# Using the Cards with Tarot Readings

If you are a tarot reader, you can use the Talisman Oracle to bring clarity to your readings, or you can help individuals create their own talismans. This practice will help querents refocus their purpose when experiencing difficulty accomplishing their vision or finding their peace.

# SPREADS

## THREE-CARD SPREADS

There are a variety of ways you can use the three-card spreads. Which version you should pick depends on the topic or issue you wish to investigate.

1. Past | 2. Present | 3. Future

1. Present Situation | 2. Possibilities or Obstacles | 3. The best course of action

1. Love | 2. Professional life | 3. Environment

1. What I want | 2. What I need | 3. How to improve

# Talisman Spread

This spread looks into the different forces that need to balance before you are able to welcome abundance into your life. First, shuffle the deck then cut it an odd number of times, preferably with your left hand, which is connected to your right side brain—the source of creativity, perception and empathy.

```
    6      2      7

    4      1      5

           3
```

**Card 1**: Subconscious feelings
**Card 2**: Possibilities or obstacles
**Card 3**: Best course of action
**Card 4**: Outside forces
**Card 5**: Your surrounding and family
**Card 6**: Driving force
**Card 7**: Future outcome

# The Cards

## ⟨ Balanced Emotions ⟩

### In a Reading

Jellyfish are graceful creatures that trust the ocean currents to take them to their destination. Take a moment to evaluate the way you spend your energy. Sometimes we cannot see the grand picture and get caught up in the moment. If we are unable to see the lesson a situation is teaching us, we can get entangled in our emotions and the need for control. Are you holding on too tightly to feelings that don't serve you well? It's easier to see the solution when you feel calmer. Find a peaceful place in your home or outside where you can spend some time allowing your emotions to exist without judgment. Take a breath, acknowledge them and let go of those that no longer support you.

## Talisman Power

Use this card when you need a step back to rebalance your position. Keep your talisman close when you are around triggers that activate you more than usual, whether that's a person, a place, or a memory. Envision the jellyfish's peaceful flow and existence every time you find yourself circling back to the negative feelings. Be mindful not to suppress this energy because it could erupt. Instead try to observe patiently and find your balance.

*I am gentle with my feelings.*

## Banish a Curse

### In a reading

This card can symbolize unfair treatment towards you. A person who has a strong influence in your life has mistreated you or fails to see your point of view. The actions of others speak for their misalignment, not yours, and you have the power to choose how that impacts you. Your worth does not change based on other people's state of mind. The pain or misunderstandings can disappear if you decide not to internalize the negativity. Dwelling over what has been said means reliving the hurtful emotion and letting it control your actions. It's time to take a step back and allow the new positive energy to embrace you. Think of what you can learn from this experience and know that karma has your back.

## Talisman Power

Use this card when you feel like you need extra help removing the bad energy lingering around you. Focus on the wheel in the center of the card; it represents the power of transformation. The swords have locked it in place and the wheel cannot move. Envision pulling each blade out and turning the wheel clockwise. The four snakes are untangling their bodies and are set free. The wheel is now moving, and the blossom in the center can draw the nourishing energy it needs. The curse is lifted!

*I am honest and worthy.*

## BLESSED DAY

### IN A READING

From sunrise to moonset, you are blessed to have good luck. If you see this card in a reading, know that today is your day to act upon your wishes. The silk moth is a symbol of internal transformation and hope. Start directing change toward what you want to achieve. It all starts with believing that you can. Joy and happiness will surround you and follow you the entire day. Spread your wings, embrace the beautiful energy and share it with the rest of the world.

## Talisman Power

Use this card when you need extra help on a specific day. For example, you can use it for special events, meetings, anniversaries, court days, or any day you need to go smoothly, full of joy and confidence. This card will lose its energy quickly, so you won't be able to use it on consecutive days. Make your choice wisely and trust its power. Every time the doubt comes back, hear, see and feel the fluttering wings of the moth.

*I am joyous.*

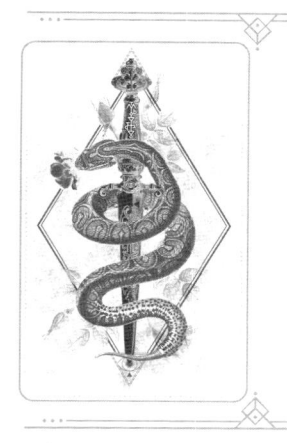

## Cast Away Negativity

### In a reading

Choose carefully your friends and the people you surround yourself with. At times you may need to temporarily distance yourself from the people who cannot see your vision and are not in a place to understand your opinion and feelings. Allow them time to grow stronger and try to see why they feel vulnerable. The rose in the snake's mouth represents kindness. Soften the negative words and thoughts by adopting a positive attitude. Consider whether it's more important to be right or to build a happy and peaceful presence. With a bit of kindness, you might be able to turn the currents in your favor. Playing games is not the path you want to take now. The sword in this card is a symbol of protective power, but also of honor and justice.

## Talisman Power

Use this card when you need to release the negative energy that may be blocking you. Keep this card near when you're trying to grow stronger and rise above the resentful eyes. Look at the snake on the card and imagine it hissing. Suddenly its tongue turns into a beautiful rose, and the snake becomes calmer and falls asleep.

*I set my boundaries with kindness.*

## CHANGE

### IN A READING

New experiences will bring excitement to your life. You will be taking a risk or unknown step forward but listen to your intuition and follow the process of change. The chameleon feels no need to rush. The best opportunity lies ahead, waiting for you. Don't fear making mistakes because they present opportunities to grow and learn something new. Acknowledge that it's a time of progress, and don't waste your energy fighting this move. The Seed of Life behind the chameleon represents the unity of all aspects of life. This change will bring cumulative fulfillment. Be ready to embrace the unknown and enjoy the adventure ahead of you.

## Talisman Power

Use this card when you are ready to step out of your comfort zone; when you are in a new environment, and you need to adapt smoothly. In a situation where you feel the fear of change rising, envision the chameleon changing its color. Assign different colors to the various energy or emotions you want to channel, and with time, remembering those colors will help you embrace that particular energy.

*I am adaptable.*

## Concealment

### IN A READING

You've taught yourself how to be strong, how to be a go-getter, and how to protect yourself. You've conquered obstacles because you know where you stand and hiding behind a mask can feel safe. When you conceal your true identity and don't let people fully know you, they can't hurt you. The glamorously painted faces look very appealing and provide a sense of shelter. However, if you keep avoiding connecting on a deeper level, it can leave you feeling vulnerable and alone. Commit to making choices that are better for your unique essence and purpose.

## Talisman Power

Use this card when you want to unmask a certain aspect of your life; if you need to reveal your true feelings or when you need to dig beneath the surface of a situation that has left you unsure of yourself. Imagine carrying the mask for a little while, and then envision yourself removing it. At first, this may be frightening and might make you feel exposed and vulnerable, but you will learn to stay stronger and forthright with practice. Try writing down on a piece of paper something positive that people don't know about you.

*I am true to myself.*

## Confidence

### IN A READING

The queen bee shows up in your reading to remind you of your stamina and the vital role you play in someone else's life. You are completely and utterly unique and your confidence and self-esteem are what make you influential. You have been chosen for your part because you have all that it takes to lead the way. Your self-confidence grows as you look for your answers through knowledge and experience. The sacrifice of short-term gratification in order to achieve long-term goals yields some of the biggest rewards. Fear of failure or even of your success is counterproductive. You know that to double your accomplishments, you need to double the number of mistakes, so don't be afraid of making a misstep.

## Talisman Power

Use this card to charge your self-confidence. Envision the power of the queen bee caring for her own needs and those of the others. See yourself rising up strong and determined.

*I am me. I am enough.*

## Courage

### In a reading

This card represents courage, will and determination. It will be through dealing with a new set of obstacles that you will make your most significant leap forward. We learn little from times of ease. The peaceful moments in life reward us for the hard work we've done, but those easy times don't give us the opportunity to show our perseverance and strength of character. You have what it takes to see this situation through to the end. Courage evolves, and it can grow into compassion, patience and forgiveness. Nevertheless, alongside the hard times in life, we can still see the joy and be present for all the goodness coming our way.

## Talisman Power

Use this when you need extra energy to overcome hardship. Visualize the lion courageously standing still. His wounds might be raw and the times scary, but the power within gives hope for a better tomorrow. Healing blooms among thorns, and the flowers' scent makes us feel relaxed and optimistic.

*I am strong.*

## CREATIVITY

### IN A READING

Spider silk is five times stronger than steel. The spider has found the most beautiful way to create a form that possesses strength, flexibility, delicacy and enticement. The Seed of Life at the top reminds us that the evolution of the creative form takes time and can be dormant before it's ready to be released into the world. At the center, you can see a pentagram with the five elements. Look for inspiration everywhere around you. This card can mean creating a project or using artistry in a delicate situation. A little bit of creativity can go a long way and can brighten your spirit and lighten up the mood. Sometimes we instinctively try to use force to make something happen; but more often, a creative approach will yield more fruitful results.

## Talisman Power

Use this card when you need to awaken your imagination and unleash your creative flow. You can also use this card when you feel you're at a dead end with an issue. Spend some time visualizing the spider weaving the web and its beautiful architecture. See the powerful energy coming from all elements and sources, and know it's speaking through you, coming to life.

*I am inventive and resourceful.*

## Cut Ties

### IN A READING

You are at the end of a path with a person, situation, or a memory that has drained your energy long enough. It's time to cut ties with what holds you back and venture back into the world to find new opportunities. You have spent enough time trying to find a solution, and dwelling over what "could and should have been" is no longer helpful. Try to see this as a new beginning, a bright moment of discovery. The two circles in the card represent the two rings of attachment—emotional and intellectual. Picture the knife cutting through both rings to release them, and yourself.

## Talisman Power

Use this card when you feel you cannot remove yourself from the clutches of unpleasant situations. Visualize a rope holding you tightly. Take the knife and imagine cutting through all of the loops with ease. Imagine taking a deep breath and the feeling of freedom. You are strong, powerful, and ready to move on.

*I cut this link in order to heal.*

## DEFENSE

### IN A READING

Watch out for competition in a personal or professional context. It's time to defend your current position, but you should have no problems doing so. While it is flattering that others strive for your success, this creates a very harsh environment, and it becomes difficult to lead within this dynamic. You are fierce, and when you want something, you go for it. Try to understand where others are coming from but do establish clear boundaries. Focus on the solution of the issue and defend your ground and ignore the empty chatter that could fuel the needless drama.

## Talisman Power

Use this card when others try to start an argument, provoke you, or challenge your success. The Scorpio is ready to set the limits, but the flowers on this card soften the tense feelings. Meditate with this card, knowing that the ill winds will blow over. The challenges placed on our path make us stronger and allow us to believe in ourselves more.

*I am unbreakable because I am at peace.*

## Destiny

### IN A READING

Social limitations and negative bias* trick our subconscious into believing we are not able to achieve our desires. We are taught to hide our unique nature to fit into the environment around us. Those coping skills keep us safe and acclimated to avoid danger, but they rob us of the power of positive manifestation. By training the mind to pay attention to the positive, we feed our subconscious mind the belief that we can create our destiny and propel ourselves forward. Our minds can be free when we use this key that we've carried on our back all along—we own the power to change the narrative.

## Talisman Power

Use this card when you need to shake the negative thoughts that are holding you back. We can't control the actions of others, but we can change our perspective. Envision having a chain of keys and trying a few to unlock the cage. How does it feel to finally find the right key? Feel the presence of the cage and armor dissolve as you notice the gentle breeze of freedom on your skin.

*I am free.*

---

*A negative bias is our tendency to remember the negative far greater than the positive. Studies show that remembering negative experiences exhibits in a ratio as little as 3-to-1 and as large as 30-to-1.

We have to make a conscious effort to override the pattern.

## DIVINE GUIDANCE

### IN A READING

It's best to watch out for a sign before moving forward. You are ready to enjoy the fruits of your hard work but don't decide to embrace any one aspect of your life just yet. Wait for some more information to emerge before making that choice. This card can also mean that it's best to use your intuition to make the final call rather than your rational mind. Try to read the signs carefully and trust your instincts. Although it may be frustrating to wait, proceeding when the time is right will be much more rewarding.

## Talisman Power

Use this card when you feel at a crossroad or when you need a sign. Self-doubt can be overpowering but waiting for the right time is necessary at this juncture. The frog stays still before getting ready to reenergize. Imagine being the frog and patiently waiting for the right moment. If waiting feels hard, try focusing your attention on all the sounds in nature the frog could be hearing.

*I am patient.*

## Elixir of Life

### In a reading

Mortality is a reminder that life is short. The Elixir of Life card does not offer immortality but shows up in a reading to remind you that there are things that are greater than us, and by adopting this philosophy, we can become part of a whole that is of itself immortal. We want both simplicity and abundance, and seeing the pure energy connecting us can be liberating. Our unconditional capacity for love and kindness is immeasurable and has the ability to remove all fear. Acknowledging the laws of nature that govern the universe places on us the power and responsibility to create our own sense of meaning.

## Talisman Power

This card can be used in a variety of ways that can best be determined by you. The Elixir of Life offers insight when you are on a quest for meaning. Meditate with this card when you need to free your mind and see the bigger picture. Imagine taking a sip of truth serum and looking within to see what makes you truly happy.

*Energy lives forever.*

# Equilibrium

## In a reading

It's time to align your intentions with your actions. You are dancing between opposite forces, and your mind is racing with ideas. The complexity of motion is important in the discovery of new methods, and when all the forces acting upon us balance each other, we are at equilibrium. Our perseverance and ability to let go coalesce in a state of harmony. Learning to accept misfortunes but having determination in the pursuit of our dreams brings confidence. The water takes whatever shape it's poured into so you can direct where the energy goes.

## Talisman Power

Harness the power of this card to direct your focus. Use it to purify energy or create a balance between body, mind, and spirit. Envision the water lifting in the air. To strengthen the belief, you can pour water from one glass to another a few times to see the visual manifestation of nature's balance.

*Energy flows where your focus goes.*

## ETERNAL CHARISMA

### IN A READING

You are captivating and have a charming personality that attracts others. You are charismatic, and you radiate with a luminous glow. You have so much to offer; believe in yourself and what you stand for, and don't be afraid to share your vision. Be a social butterfly and make connections with others as you pursue your dreams.

Channel your strength but don't be scared to show your vulnerability. Eternal charisma forms within. It is not defined by money or age. Charismatic souls are genuinely interested in the people around them and make everyone feel special.

## Talisman Power

Meditate with this card when you need to recharge your energy before or after a busy social event. Often, an overwhelming crowd can drain our batteries and leave us in a mood for quiet time with a good book and a blanket. You can also use this card when you feel self-conscious, or when you want to focus on your appearance. See yourself as the butterfly that helps flowers open up and bloom, spreading the positive energy from flower to flower while drinking the sweet nectar of delight.

*I attract others.*

## FINANCIAL SECURITY

### IN A READING

You are about to experience great rewards or success concerning financial security. This card can indicate a sudden blessing or the feeling of finally advancing in your career. Complete success in a financial partnership lies ahead. You will be lucky in your investments and won't have to worry about your lifestyle. This doesn't mean you can be reckless with your spending, but it's time to treat yourself a little. There are four moons on this card, indicating the results you seek are not instantaneous, but your deliberate, calculated risks will turn out favorable, as four is the number of stability.

## Talisman Power

Use this card to attract luck in your financial endeavors, and when you need to be creative about your finances. Imagine the roots of the coin going deeper into the ground, and like a seed of security, it is now planted and safe. With time, the plant will blossom and flourish.

*I am strategic.*

## Finding Love

### In a reading

A pure, conscious connection is awaiting you. This card doesn't always represent instant chemistry in an intimate relationship. It could also represent a nourishing platonic bond based on honesty and mutual appreciation. As this card also means finding your true soulmate, be on the lookout as serendipity can bring an inevitable shift in the air that can form a spark in your love life. A stable and fulfilling connection built on trust and respect can make you fascinated with your other half, but moreover, it helps you reconnect with your true self.

## Talisman Power

Seahorses mate for life. Meditate with this card when you want to strengthen your relationship with your beloved. If you are single, you can also use this card to find a companion who understands and encourages you. Be cautious not to use this card for a relationship that ignites a fire that burns everything in its way. True love does not make you second guess your honesty, loyalty, or your self-worth. Believe in the magic because it's here for you!

*I embody love.*

## Good Fortune

### IN A READING

In ancient Egypt, the Scarab beetle was a symbol of good fortune, rebirth, and protection from jealousy. This card indicates prosperity and long-term success. It could also mean a miracle or a blessing. This, however, is not a passive fortune. Now is the time to formulate new ideas about the path you want to follow. Decide what you are interested in and take action because luck is on your side. This card can ease the hard work that needs to be done to get to the finish line, but it's up to you to see yourself through. You will resurrect your power when you encounter obstacles on your way, but you need to stay focused on your goals. Don't forget to celebrate your success.

## Talisman Power

The Good Fortune card can be used in numerous ways, all tied in with long-lasting good fortune. Use this card when you want to find your calling or when you want to increase the long-term beneficial effect in a relationship, business venture, or situation. Envision the scarab beetle digging around and gathering good luck.

*I attract good fortune.*

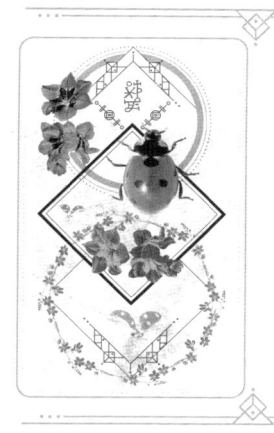

## Good Luck

### IN A READING

Luck is with you and with everything you touch! This is a very positive card that indicates growth and increased potential. The currents are in your favor, and if you act upon your wishes, you will benefit greatly. It's up to you to channel this good fortune. The circles on the card form the number eight. Eight is an auspicious number and a symbol of new beginnings. Fate will take a strong hand and redirect your path in a very positive way. What you do after this shift is in your own hands.

## Talisman Power

Use this card when you need a little extra stardust for your projects and ventures. You can also use this card if you're feeling a bit short of luck. Imagine the circles spinning slowly and the ladybug fluttering around the flowers. You are attracting them, and you feel their tickling feet landing in your hand and the magic swirling all around.

*I attract good luck.*

## Grounding

### In a reading

The anchor in this card represents grounding and stability. A long-awaited relationship, position, or financial compensation will become permanent. You can now ease your mind and focus on the desired security. This card can mean finally seeing the light after a challenging period. The stormy weather is over, and you can now adjust to the new steady pace in life. Don't be afraid to take a chance, but choose the option with long-term beneficial results if the opportunity arises.

## Talisman Power

Use this card when you need grounding or stability in your fast-paced environment. This card can also offer spiritual grounding when emotions are running wild. Look at the card and picture the anchor slowly moving through the water and reaching the ocean bottom. The light coming from the lighthouse shines brightly to show you that you have nothing to fear, and you are finally home.

*I know I am safe and secure.*

## Growth of Energy

### In a reading

You have been very productive and organized, trying to prepare for the next step in life. Your creativity is flowing, you have built a nest, and as you look at your potential, the future no longer seems frightening. Everything is in its place, and you are growing the energy for a big new project. The six petals in the "Seed of Life" signify that a blessing is on your path, and you have to take care and nurture your ideas to see them come to life. This newfound energy is bubbling up, and your excitement is lighting up the room. Don't be surprised if people compliment your looks because of your radiant spirit. This card could also mean pregnancy or childbirth.

## Talisman Power

Use this card when you are ready to start a new stage in life or a new project requiring a lot of attention and energy. You can also use this card when you are launching a new business. Envision the eggs snuggled cozily together in their nest. They are safe and sound, and they are growing every day. It's slow and tedious work that needs a lot of patience, but you've got this!

*I am ready for this new adventure.*

## Happiness

### IN A READING

It's time to appreciate life with a bright and positive outlook. We all go through difficulties, but when the waters are finally still, we can fill our hearts with gratitude and radiate the joy from what we have accomplished. Cherish every moment and shine brightly! The flower in the center of this card is soaking up the abundant positive energy from the two suns and forms nourishing and delightful seeds. Practicing mindfulness and inner gratitude can open a new world for you, full of compassion, love, clarity and joy. Radiate your energy and share your gift with others. Receiving people's help can bring you as much happiness as helping others. Don't be surprised if the joy becomes contagious.

## Talisman Power

Use this card when you have a hard time reconnecting with nature or appreciating the little things. Or, if you feel a bit down and you need a refreshing new outlook on life. Imagine the two suns on the card shining bright. One sun lives inside us, and the other is a mirror reflection—smile, and it will smile back. See the petals of the sunflower gently flutter. You are safe under the warmth of this card. The card's energy is so intense it becomes hot to the touch.

*I am grateful for life.*

## HEALING ENERGY

### IN A READING

Take a moment to reconnect with your true self. It's time to heal the wounds you might carry, dissolve the stress, and replace the negative energy blocking your radiant character. Little insecurities can become trigger points, so it's time to affirm our values and embrace our quirks. Sometimes, self-examination can be scary and upsetting, but it also brings joy and rebirth. Healing deeper scars doesn't mean that the pain or harm never existed, but it will no longer control your actions. This tree is anchored and is absorbing the energy from the Transmutation Circle. You own the power of your own transformation, and you, too, can blossom with lush energy.

## Talisman Power

Use this card when you feel drained and in need of healing power. Meditate with this card by envisioning growing roots similar to a tree going deep in the ground, tapping into the vast energy that the world is made of. Imagine luminous veins growing on you, reaching every part of your body. Your heart and your mind are now shining brighter. The light radiates out of your body and out into space.

*I am healing.*

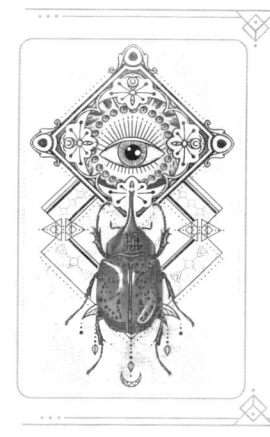

## INTUITION

### IN A READING

You are wide awake and able to perceive a higher level of awareness that helps you recognize secrets and subconscious intentions. The intuitive beetle is using the third eye gate to see through the prism of distortion. The answers you are seeking will come from within—from your divine knowledge and inner wisdom. Your intuition will help you read people's body language and facial expressions if they are in disagreement with their words and actions. Allow time and space to practice putting your newly found feelings into words but know that your present situation will benefit significantly from your keen intuition.

## Talisman Power

Use this card to strengthen your intuitive ability and psychic insight. Meditate with this card when you feel your instincts rising in a tricky situation. Focus on this image to awaken your third eye and enter the realm of your higher consciousness. Rub your forehead gently and imagine opening up your third eye.

*I am awake, and I see.*

## Karmic Justice

### In a reading

If you seek the balance of karma, then this card is a positive sign that whatever the outcome of a particular situation, it will be a fair one. Karmic justice doesn't look the same for everyone because we have different values and desires. Don't expect the repercussions to be immediate or of the same nature; they will be of equal worth. However, if your own efforts have been unfair, this card could also mean that it's time to accept the consequences. Put bias and prejudice aside and open your heart. The endless knot on this card symbolizes wisdom, compassion and balance in the universe.

## Talisman Power

Use this card when you seek justice. When injustice happens, it can be hard to recognize the pattern in nature that will rebalance the unfair act. Justice will be served, but it is no longer in your hands. The beetles on this card are about to receive equal results if they both pull the lever with equal strength. Imagine the movement of this abstract scale coming into balance.

*The energy we spend is the energy we receive.*

## KNOWLEDGE

### IN A READING

Knowledge is a powerful tool that can open the doors to opportunities and freedom. It is an ongoing process to better ourselves and grow. It takes courage and strength to admit when we don't understand something, and we need to seek more information. Our doubt is not a final destination. We can turn it into a willingness to grow and evolve, or to change our circumstances. Following this path of learning can bring fulfillment and confidence that there is a solution to every problem. We can detect enthusiasm and hope for a brighter future because we own the power of mastering ourselves.

## Talisman Power

Use this card when you seek educational opportunities, when studying for exams, conducting research, or when you are looking for a breakthrough in an academic field. Imagine the lamp glowing brighter over the book, the pages start turning, and the light shines on just the right paragraph you need. The smell of the fresh bouquet brings a sense of hope and brightens the mood.

*I seek knowledge.*

## LEADERSHIP

### IN A READING

You have been placed in a situation where you have to take the lead. This newfound responsibility can be frightening, but it offers you an opportunity to see your vision come to life. Set boundaries and focus on the bigger picture. You are able to brighten up the spirit of those around you, and you see their potential. You have the confidence, decisiveness, empathy, and insight that inspires others. In the course of your life, you have gained valuable experience and respect, and now it's your chance to offer guidance. Ego battles are no match for you. You have mastered self-discipline and creative humor and have let go of the need to micromanage the small stuff.

## Talisman Power

Use this card whenever you need help believing in your leadership skills. You can also use it when you experience difficulties as a parent or head of a social group or organization. Envision the stamina of the tiger and channel his firm but gentle spirit. Take a few deliberate steps ahead and allow the doubts to dissolve.

*I offer guidance.*

## LEARN THE TRUTH

### IN A READING

We are human, and our nature is prone to error. But those errors are opportunities to grow and master a new skill. Sometimes we are unable to see the truth because we compete with ourselves. Our ego doesn't let us move forward because first, we have to acknowledge our own shortcomings. You know what you have to do, and it's time to sit with the uncomfortable feelings. It's okay if it doesn't feel familiar because progress happens when we step away from our comfort zone. The truth can be so liberating; see the opportunities that weren't there when you had your eyes closed. The owl will be your guide through the darkness.

## Talisman Power

Use this card when you seek the truth. Meditate on the images when you feel overpowered by a choice you need to make and need clarity. Envision a dark but warm place, see the owl landing right next to you. He is friendly and brings gifts—the fruit of clarity. He wants your attention. Where will he go next? Follow him and discover what path is best for you.

*My flaws helped me grow, and now I see the truth.*

## Let Go

### IN A READING

Just like running water, everything keeps constantly changing. You've been holding onto a burden that's been slowing you down. Sometimes we know what that is; other times, we need to examine our needs and behavior. Often holding on comes from a need to control our life and surroundings. It gives us comfort that we can direct the circumstances and avoid a painful path. But if we let go of the illusion of control, we can find peace and enjoy the ride. Being vulnerable offers an opportunity for connection and closure. The little crab has to learn to let things go. The flower in front of him is a delicate gift from nature to bring joy.

## Talisman Power

Use this card when you need to let go. The burden is too heavy, and your tiny claws are clutching with tremendous effort. Take a breath; on inhale, form fists with your hands and hold them as tight as you can. On exhale, open your hands, release the negative energy and feel the powerful relief.

*I release this energy.*

# Luna

## IN A READING

This card represents the freedom of desire and the illuminated path of moonlit dreams. The night can bring comfort to let your imagination fly and to show your wild side. In the dark, our subconscious can bring to the surface vivid clues of a hidden situation. You can achieve your goals and desires if you pay close attention to the limitations of logic and reason. This card can also represent prophetic dreams and the unrealized wild side that calls upon you.

## Talisman Power

Use the Luna card to conjure some moon magic and to evoke prophetic dreams, epiphanies, and your imagination. You can also use this card if you're having trouble sleeping. Our bodies are made of 60% water, and we know that the moon affects the water levels tremendously. Meditate with this card, preferably by gazing out at the moon. This celestial body has the power to induce our subconscious dreams. Try telling her your deepest wishes and inspirations.

After you state your wish say:

*And so it will be.*

## Magical Power

### In a reading

We are born with a special gift of magic. We often overlook this extraordinary power to bring happiness to those around us or into our own hearts. In the center of it all is a very powerful emotion—love. By setting up our intent, we can create a new world. Believing in ourselves begins with loving and being kind to who we are, understanding our limits, and pushing just a little further to better ourselves. In these ways we become closer to fulfilling our purpose in life. The dragonflies start their life as larvae in water and later rise up into the air and fly. They are our connection with nature and our guides to the realm of magic.

## Talisman Power

Use this card to strengthen your intent or awaken your magical gift. You can use the Magical Power card with any other card to enhance the potential of its meaning. Focus on the magical hexagram and the powerful energy that spreads on the card. Feel the charge of life feeding your ability. The dragonfly lifts itself into the air and flies away. Follow the winged messenger!

*The magic is me!*

## MINDFULNESS

### IN A READING

There is a lot of beauty in the stillness of the mind. Allowing ourselves to be present in the moment and not worry about how things could have been or what we could have done better can open our minds to the treasures of what we have to be thankful for. With great patience and perseverance, we can accomplish anything. It's best not to rush into action or judgment too quickly. Often patience is not about how long we can wait but what we do with our time while waiting. We can learn to be grateful for every moment of our day, even when we feel stuck, and things don't go our way. Like the praying mantis, staying mindful will make all of your endeavors mere fruitful and meaningful.

## Talisman Power

Use this card when you need to recenter and find peace in the moment. When you have a hard time being patient with yourself, try taking a moment to envision the praying mantis staying still. Bring your hands to center and focus on your breath. Can you locate where in your body your emotions are resonating? Is something tense? What sounds do you hear around you?

*I am still.*

## NAVIGATION

### IN A READING

It's time to tap into your innate navigation system and plan your trip. Determine where you are heading and imagine the final destination where you see yourself at peace. After all, even the best GPS wouldn't do you any good if you don't know the address. Determine where you are right now in your life, clarify your vision and check what attitudes will help you along the way. Forming a new healthy habit doesn't come easily, but you can prevail with a strong will and determination. This card can also symbolize finding your calling and purpose in life.

## Talisman Power

Use this card when you want to better visualize your goals. The universe has a magical way of manifesting when we truly present our desire. Imagine yourself in the murky waters; your internal compass is here to navigate you through the mud and difficulties. See yourself going through the seaweed and into the clear waters, where your destination is right in front of you. It's here waiting for you.

*This is my goal.*

Or, state your goal in a very concise sentence.

## OVERCOME FEAR

### IN A READING

The unknown can be frightening, and it's easy for those feelings to intensify in the darkness or when we feel exhausted. Make sure all of your needs are met and you are well-rested. It takes patience, consistency, and validation to rewire the old paths of your thoughts. Perhaps a past experience is triggering the current emotions, so acknowledge the reasons you feel this way. Note the way you speak to yourself. You are strong and powerful, and you can overcome anything but also remember to be gentle and patient with who you are. Move slowly at your own pace and see yourself shining in the bright, warm light of this glowing candle.

## Talisman Power

Use this card when you need to face your fears or anxiety. Create a safe space in your mind by imagining lighting a candle. The candle represents your bravery, and the prickly branches on this card are your fears and anxiety. Look at the card again and envision the light shining brighter and stronger until it spills over the edges of the card and out in reality. Feel the burden dissolve and notice how light this new feeling of love and trust becomes.

*I can manage my feelings.*

## Passion

### IN A READING

Allow your passion to rise up. Sometimes we try to suppress our desires to fit the social expectations and norms, but we can use this powerful force to thrive in a personal or professional matter. Our passion for life is immense because it comes from a place of love. This feeling is the ultimate and most powerful energy that we can emit. Be passionate about what you do and believe. Do not carry out decisions based on fear, worry, guilt or shame. That state of mind can only bring the same type of negative feelings back to you. Choose the best version of yourself and project that passion out into the universe.

## Talisman Power

Use this card when you need to strengthen your beliefs, elevate your thought frequency, and project your passion. This card can be combined with Eternal Charisma or Finding Love to increase passion in your love life. Spend some time envisioning your ideals and goals, and then go for it!

*Love is powerful.*

## Protection

### In a reading

You are divinely protected. The scary door knocker in the center of this card is here to protect you. Cast away the darkness, and bring good fortune and health to you, your home, and your family. Spend some time with this card to feel its power. Imagine the force field that radiates outward and expands as you strengthen your intent. You are shielded in this dome, and all the negative energy, curses, and bad wishes bounce off of it. If a negative vibe approaches, your energy shines bright and powerful and quickly repels it. Embrace and comfort your inner child that was left longing. You are safe in this time and space.

## Talisman Power

Use the Protection card if you feel setbacks are happening around you. You can use this card when you start living in a new home and you want to cleanse the negative energy. Meditating on this card can be very powerful if you combine it with a ritual of your own—burning sage, lighting a candle, or performing water rituals. It might feel silly but try making a scary face and voice of your own. Scare the bad energy away.

*I am sheltered.*

## Rebirth

### IN A READING

This card could be very positive in a reading. The rebirth card symbolizes the end of one period and the beginning of another. This card could also represent the release of a bad habit, unhealthy attachment, struggle, or the end of a vicious cycle. The moth is born at the end of a period of painful growth, and it's now able to fly. Energy never dissipates; it only changes from one form to another. But if you resist leaving behind the old path, you may experience some distress. Try to see the positive energy coming at you and the opportunity you are being given. Leaving something behind and looking back could bring nostalgia and longing for the old days, but the future holds a different role for you. It's time to face it and start your bright new beginning!

## Talisman Power

You can use this card when you are in a transitional period, when you need to move or start a new job or say goodbye to the past. Meditate with this card to set your new intention. This is a delicate time, and you need to be patient and kind to yourself. Imagine a tingling sensation on your skin. It's gentle, like fluttering wings but quite strong and moves like a wave to the center of your body. As it's moving away from you, at first, it forms a sphere, and then it slowly takes its own shape. What do you see?

## Resilience

### In a reading

There might be a task you have to undertake that will be difficult, unpleasant, or inconvenient. It may affect other people's feelings, but you are obliged to first make sure that you are safe and provided for. When our physical needs are not met, elevating the mind and soul can sound impossible. Use your positive attitude and steady temperament to avoid focusing on feelings of guilt or doubt. Dealing with adversity makes us more resilient, and it does the same for others. We cannot shield our loved ones from difficulties, but we can be there to hold their hand and offer our understanding and empathy. You are making the right move!

## Talisman Power

Use this card when you need to stay sharp and clever. This is not a card to use for deceit, but it's about becoming mindfully cunning and finding a creative way to provide for your own needs. Imagine the clever fox finding and learning the ways around the hunter traps. Look for ideas all around.

*I am resilient.*

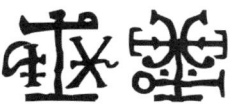

## SAFE TRAVEL

### IN A READING

You are on a journey into the unknown. You are in search of new or expanded understanding of yourself, others, nature, or a higher good. This experience opens your mind and lets you see a part of the puzzle you never knew existed. This card can mean it's time to take a pilgrimage, travel abroad, or an inner journey of introspection. This act is of great importance in knowing who you are and the meanings you are looking for. This card can mean a metaphorical journey into your own beliefs. It might be time to discover the constraints of the limiting thoughts we sometimes impose on ourselves. The Arctic tern, a wise and experienced traveler, will guide you towards the shore.

## Talisman Power

Use this card before travel and when you take a journey to discover your beliefs. Imagine your soul lifting up from your body and being free to fly. Where will it go; who will it meet?

*I am ready for this journey.*

## SUCCESS

### IN A READING

You have planted the seeds of success, and the stars are in your favor, gently guiding your way forward. Trust that through the storms and heavy rain, this seed will grow and prosper. Forget the feelings of doubt. You are about to achieve significant accomplishments, and it's been you alone who has done all the work. This is a well-deserved success, and when the victory comes, it cannot be taken away. Enjoy!

## Talisman Power

This card brings great optimism for the future of any given project or issue. Use it with a specific subject in mind. Look at the little sprout on the card. It's deriving its energy from the star above. It is written in the sky that the small plant will flourish, and it's up to you to nurture and patiently await its blooms.

*My efforts are fruitful.*

## Union

### In a reading

This card represents unity, wholeness, and fulfillment. Harmony can arise from forces that can be seen as opposite, yet they are interconnected, and they work to complement each other. This card can represent friendship, teamwork, or partnership. It's not essential to master every talent, skill, or knowledge because our unity with like-minded people can bring the best end results. This card teaches us to trust others and their area of expertise. The heavy weight of responsibility can be divided, and the celebration of success is much sweeter when it's shared.

## Talisman Power

Use this card to strengthen the bond in a friendship or partnership. Though rhinos sometimes live in solitude, they form crashes that are crucial to the group's survival and beneficial to the individual members. Channel the Union's strength and energy created by envisioning holding hands with your team or standing strong together as an indestructible crash.

*We are stronger together!*

## Willpower

### In a reading

It's time to channel your willpower through fierce dedication. You have set your objectives, and by applying discipline, commitment and courage, you will achieve your goals. At times your target may seem too far away, or people might try to convince you to adjust your expectations, but you alone know the power that you hold within. Stay confident in your abilities and focus on the next step in front of you. The dominant presence of the bull is helping you through the tests of your strength and resilience. The victory is within reach!

## Talisman Power

Use this card to strengthen your willpower. Sometimes stress and unpleasant circumstances can drain our energy, and in those moments, we need a little help to see our inner power. Withdraw to a quiet and personal space and focus on the bull on this card. The crown hangs heavy and yet majestic. Whisper your goal out loud and stay strong.

*I persevere!*

# Wisdom

## In a reading

The power of the mind has no limits. Wisdom is not only about having all the information and knowledge but about applying what we know to our situation so that it adds meaning and promotes the common good. This card reminds you that it's time to live life in such a way that builds the spirit. The octopus on this card is upside down, and it invites you to look for alternative perspectives to broaden your vision. Sometimes all it takes is to distance ourselves from the situation to see more clearly what's best for us and everyone we love. Your third eye is awakened and focused on the scene, so don't be afraid to look for a new viewpoint.

## Talisman Power

Use this card when looking for a new perspective or solution or when it's hard to come to terms with the outcome of a situation. Focus on this card and try to see your challenge as a witness or audience in a theatre. How do you feel about what is at hand? Sometimes literally hanging upside down can help bring a new train of thought. Try it!

*I use the wisdom within!*

# About the Creator

Nora Paskaleva is originally from Bulgaria. She moved to the USA to pursue higher education. She received her Bachelor's degree at City College of New York in Graphic Design and her Master's degree at Touro Graduate School of Technology in Web Design and Multimedia. She currently works as an Art Director in Connecticut and is a mother of two. She loves to do digital art and crafts in her free time in addition to hiking and spending time in nature.

**Visit us:**

Instagram: @talisman_thoughts
Facebook: @talismanthoughts
TikTok: @talisman_thoughts

**www.talismanthoughts.com**

# Symbols

**These symbols (or others) can be used for creating your own talismans**

| Symbol | Meaning | Symbol | Meaning |
|---|---|---|---|
| ◆ | Origin from which all start; idea; soul | ⊻ | Symbiosis, purity, support, protection |
| ⊙ | The eye of God/ The Universe | ⊥ | Protection, binding power |
| — | Flow of life and energy | □ | World, nature, four elements |
| ∣ | Higher good/ power | ◎ | Trinity of mind, body and spirit |
| ⌐ | Justice and integrity | ✡ | Balance of masculine and feminine, magic |
| ✚ | Universe and earth are in harmony | ⚭ | Love, unity, oneness |
| △ | Feminine energy, fruitfulness, fluidity, creativity | ⛧ | Time, essence, dimensions |
| ▽ | Masculine energy, logic, protection, certainty | ∼ | Instinct, intuition, free will, ancestral knowledge |
| Y | Nature / Intellect; Combine force of good and necessary bad | Ψ | Indestructible matter, strength |
| ⩓ | Growth, rank, awakening | ⳨ | Fierce dedication, focus, manpower |

# Astrological Symbols

| | | | | |
|---|---|---|---|---|
| Air | Earth | Fire | Water | |

| | | | | |
|---|---|---|---|---|
| Aries | Taurus | Gemini | Cancer | Leo |
| Virgo | Sagittarius | Libra | Scorpio | Capricorn |
| Aquarius | Pisces | Retrograde | Moon | Mars |
| Mercury | Jupiter | Venus | Saturn | Earth |
| Uranus | Neptune | Pluto | Ceres | Pallas |

For our complete line of tarot decks, books, meditation cards, oracle sets, and other inspirational products please visit our website:

**www.usgamesinc.com**

Follow us

U.S. GAMES SYSTEMS, INC.
179 Ludlow Street
Stamford, CT 06902 USA
203-353-8400
Order Desk 800-544-2637
FAX 203-353-8431